Here is rare beauty, a delirium of lan                          ıstract
pitched and wounded critique. Mute                          ıks in
word ravishments that send me to th                          ıvious,
reconsider the ordinary—like Cow, Reu, ~~Deⅲ, ⅲuⅱuaⅲ . . . ⅰ Uⅳⅽ,~~ ⅰ Took.
Harpo stammers compulsively in Justice, for Justice, as here they might meet up
in Kant's Kingdom of Ends: "Being nests its midst in me." Here is a solid iron
made malleable and the deep terrors of groundlessness . . . an intellectual verbal
allegory of air with Venus poised shaky on the half shell. Vertigo professes
through a glass darkly that at first hinges on underlying/outlying shames
but then rises to meet the eye and clear the palate of the senses—with keen
attention. And though NOT ENOUGH stands on the back of EVEN LESS in
shrouds of awful bleakness, attempts at smugness repeatedly fail. And Reality
puzzles. And Will puzzles. What is accuracy, where is truth? Harpo stands
before the opus and says flat out: *I allege a norm compels*

Karen Garthe
Author of **the haunt Road**, **The Banjo Clock**, **Frayed escort**


The most cutting thing a Roman poet could be told was that their work smelled
like the lamp. The smell of soot was the smell of labor and, by inference, of the
lack of talent. Whether or not inspiration is truly eaten by effort, the criterion
has largely damned what it meant to praise. Poems are an undertaking (the
source, in Greek, of their name), an undertaking that is skillfully completed by
a minimum of sweat. This view of poetry, as something added to the world, has
been all too convincing. But what if poetry were something else? These poems
are that something else. They are the latent patterns of sand on sand within a
dune. In a world that has already been given far more than it can survive, it is
well worth imitating these examples of impossible excavation.

lazenby
Author of **Infinity to Dine**

# Harpo Before the Opus

# Harpo Before the Opus

## Logan Fry

selected by Srikanth Reddy as winner of
the Omnidawn 1st/2nd Book Prize

OMNIDAWN PUBLISHING
OAKLAND, CALIFORNIA
2019

Cover art: Matthew Paladino
"Troys Lament," 40" x 30" x 4"
Acrylic and plaster on panel, 2016
matthewpalladino.com

Cover and interior set in Quicksand and OFL Sorts Mill Goudy

Cover and interior design by Gillian Olivia Blythe Hamel

Printed in the United States
by Books International, Dulles, Virginia
On 55# Glatfelter B19 Antique
Acid Free Archival Quality Recycled Paper

Library of Congress Cataloging-in-Publication Data

Names: Fry, Logan, 1988- author.
Title: Harpo before the opus / Logan Fry.
Description: Oakland, California : Omnidawn Publishing, 2019.
Identifiers: LCCN 2019013946 | ISBN 9781632430748 (pbk. : alk. paper)
Classification: LCC PS3606.R925 H38 2019 | DDC 811/.6--dc23
LC record available at https://lccn.loc.gov/2019013946

Published by Omnidawn Publishing, Oakland, California
www.omnidawn.com    (510) 237-5472   (800) 792-4957
10 9 8 7 6 5 4 3 2 1
ISBN: 978-1-63243-074-8

# CONTENTS

"What is a shape / Except resistance," Logan Fry asks himself, and the poems of
*Harpo Before the Opus*—in all their prosodic diversity, technical and historical
lexicons, and affective topographies—may be read as the literary manifesto for
a resistance movement of one. Yet Fry also shows us how resistance may be
grounded, all too often, in unacknowledged complicities. "I was taught to frag
then surplus," writes this disillusioned insurgent, a little sadly, in retrospect. It
could be a line from some modern-day sequel to Duck Soup; Fry conscripts
Karl into his personal pantheon of Marx Brothers, but he wryly names his book
for the one who keeps mum.

Raiding political theory to adumbrate a social economy of form, *Harpo Before
the Opus* demonstrates, in every line, how "form honors labor's waste." One
need only trace the virtuosic involutions of syntax and lineation in a passage
like this to register the labor (and waste) required to engineer innovations in
verse:

Whatever's further inner
is deeper
not because in possession of more depth
but because the framing of its presence
is so greater
the encumbrance of sensing
is kept truer
because so well impaired.

To sense "whatever's further inner" is an urgent and ancient endeavor,
shared by poets, monks, and psychoanalysts alike. Fry makes it new again by
extending philosophical inquiry, with equal measures of wit and sorrow, into
an examination of one's own systemic privilege. "Being white," he ruefully
admits, "I / was granted naming rights / to norms." Nonetheless, the searching
inquiry into the poetics of power throughout *Harpo Before the Opus* also turns
up moments of genuine grace and illumination. "Being nests its midst in me,"
observes the poet, almost startled by the fledgling hope within. Such plenitude
of being holds open the possibility of companionship, and perhaps even
comradeship. "When I ask for your hand," writes this disenchanted descendant
of Whitman, "I really / Mean it."

Srikanth Reddy, Judge of the
Omnidawn 1st/2nd Poetry Book Contest

*for Caroline*

*Tricksters or fakes, assistants or 'toons, they are the exemplars of the coming community.*

GIORGIO AGAMBEN

*The crab fishermen don't even want all the crab...they want money...*

CHELSEY MINNIS

*The artist should not want to be right.*

PHILIP GUSTON

I cold solder allure.

To limp forts cured in leisure.

Soft aperçu to bask in.

Fronds lain on a casket.

Good, it has momentum. Its horror
                    canoe glides in us,
                    such is value years
restore. Such is war that founders is
unworn. The was that founders has
is ours, is was momentum behind its
gruel that were a face slopped on; be
was a face has is place. Odor locates.
Does rise daisies when a silver runs
among maps that, over, calve facéd

traumas. These is
are living wounds.

That's the gap that the past has pulled blood thru.
That's filial, the prince's joke's splayed in the harp's croon.
Being glossy from a hung bit's haltered for youth.
In nuce, the plaster got wet again. Good look, say the dead,

let the debtors in.
Polite, knives whit
un purses, that, I, I,
worsened, as what
Kant's hems missed—
they left in stitches stitches. *We're* to equip the snitches?

I get it. Warsaw I saw in image a time. War's what I saw.
Under whose flag can I limping slip this memo?

I get it I get it. Yourhustle don'tever gounnoticed baby-I'm
w/ you I'm. With it, the grand credit ledger takes water, says
Thank you,
resumes its conversation,
thinkpiece workshopping *Cryptocurrency and the Figure of
the 20th Century Comedy Director*, it's a working title, it is in
debate, whether to swap "Father" in, the utility of it, it is a
teachable generational moment, it has decided, it is parched,
It's these meds. It looks beyond the window and the many

passing windows beyond it. It's a time-bound pose it holds.

The Composing Ledger enfolds.
*Beauty's foot* incurs synchronicity
and the nuisance of blather, arty

24

pillows arranged tall by the broker,
coffees, just coffees, set out and around, it's so gauche, only
cousins will come. It's how it wants it. I cast off the cloud I

broke in twain. Out its memory's ethos a datum tumbles.
It's encrypted. This, among others, is a benefit of slaying.
Wet, thru billows where, once, forestry built lives' facets,
*The Pragmatist's Dunebuggy* hurtles. Its driver is buoyant,
she sputters at towers districts fell about, considers the net
credit civilians let on
the glass fondant so gleamy, so ultimately
a public works, the whole project of debt, how

to have slain what one's slewn is another benefit of slaying.

The ridges on *Beauty's foot* accidently enfold the dead clouds.
Within there are gardens. To till them's how data is found.

In the list of public goods
is the prince's joke and is
Kant's paltry sewing and
is the pedant's tire swing.
Is the nuptial's trick knee
and debt's gay thinkpiece
and is the loyalist's id and
is Galileo's wet red bowel.

The way out of a memory wound
is to wound you.  It's the absence
of lack I push data thru. Color too.
Pain's litany's form is the feedback loop, which hoops yr plangence,
a bust of hastening, and which leaps against doing, the seawall of it.
Being heaps beside it.
There are a few still, loose piles where the datalogged bodies drift.

Preserve the painting under dirt, sure. I'd keep
a foot slung over the fence
I were you...
Yours are sources rifts wear in opalescent film.

Time so loves its lacquer.

If one is to confab weather,
surface will do. Plus, what's not weather,
bend in closer,
loose the atoms slough over a departure.

A river is only to make time livid.

Some gaunt hunt gave us runes

To sharpen love's ardor

Love affords gore

Somehow cored hours melt out

While a forge buffers a calculus

'Things' go 'up' so

Sore ratios bruise better vectors

To ascend peaks to tally each up

Atop is where rigor

Weighs its pouring

If in lather a count foams toward

Cure will

Approximate doing

To go toward is pure but

Is urge the purest good of cusps

Lifting an

Arm lifting a hand lifting

Data into where the air's thinned

Bend any feeling inward

Enough it fends off limit

That grave archive

Longing burdens thorough air of

This is the first of many fondles.

About one's dullish being limbs
Appear / Silly.
Fetch them. Thanks.

Heavy is *The Fiat's Dustup* where it thrums.
It thrums like any loaded gun, it bends the
Air's ethos in
To where its killing's curled.

The poor need not the worry say not the poor.
That worry needs the poor what need the not.

"Soon enough," some
  Continue to say even when it's long been later.

The plainness of telling is wetwork.
Cast later, then nearer,
Time wills tells forward.
The abundance of truth is no levee.

I admit I harvest precision from love.
Lear was precious about rending.
That doesn't bud sublimates our trust
Norms use to lure a fig from ripeness.

Orange can be
softer theorem

if a wet cant is

taken upon it
further upon a

cast air left red

Goethe follow
yellow reason

nails wont rut
in that note I

posted, affixed
with the torque

your litmus had.

However gifted.

Being nests its midst in me
sallow fain in plainness' arc
toward heft a laming tense
cusps with, and so before I

found a mold to foam up if
caring tare one would zero
out the use of, gassing furs
that consign languish to evade how ripe the terror is.

The heat evaluates its find
policing as a genre bearing
out pustules rubbed so for
to lance them. Ought flints

when a reason's its supply
and guts a longer sense of
proper life one's custodial
need becoming's laurels drape alongside fear's mists.

I strive then toward a like
I mean toward likeness as
a fact I give to it in a dank
hope to lure an ease forth

before a task I took a limp
where placid, lamping war
open so to lash it up then.
A need belittles twenty times the league u place it in.

Well orange had by then well

tethered me to the underside of

pain as well as pushed at some

the edges I had by then built

within what I then thought myself

to be, in praise of shadow, adoring

shadow for the light atop it, then.


I lack the worth to tell this,

shapes gain color over time but

underneath that there's some other,

most unknown dimension gliding thru

that plane. I've called it, reaching, scent

before, but that's wrong too. Somehow


knowing a thing holds the think like so,

like how it is

by a faculty above pure memory

that permanence figures into it,

stability of form encased in quality,

finding qua in the hollow places

one stashes along their route more into.


Giving. Into. Those and others purge source

from tributary, contributing to the silt that

dearth had left on lack,

a sickly sensing— Not of scent—

but a thing felt

at the berm of knowing.

I allege a norm compels what's

verdant and thereby before us.

I feed the crocodiles bark.
Sure as destiny is porous
the need for pureness lists toward
the cliff under grievance,
a grove citrus leaves won't prune.

Utopia could settle over any place.
An idea is so called for its lag
tugging at the roiling airiness
of speech. I lean with a fat piece
of lemon bark over the fence.
Grace could settle over any place.

Lewd is a gross of human asks.
In low voice, what pools sates.

If I bend it is a textbook index.
I buy twine by the bushel. I am
business, a plump discernment.
My whole task is in deeming to.

Below acuity rests a gestated oil.
One good sear flesh tears a gain.

I nimble a tool into depth's edge.
I care for tremor as I do my trick.
If not felt in alloy this fells acres.
Loam incurs qua as perilous fact.

I soothe torn land with leitmotif.
Needly features become the cue.
I relax pouring Casper into vases.
Hot woe leers its gushes through.

Ruin fixed permanent in me

care for its public's take dismissed

plastic as the ocean

and from a higher tuft its flakes

sift through to compile

by rational degrees. The city leaks.

About the seal's foundation's knowing's pique.

Gentlemen get addressed and tan

by credit's hearth I'm tasked to hurl

logs in. Then there's this

task force that was formed to garner loss

and file it and forget

where the file went. I forge them

in my free time I accumulate in cubic grains

then sift, sort, and allot by use of Shift plus

left parenthesis

plus "the" Insert, then I use it all in thinking up

new formats to foresee the data pile in.

"Public" I would say's misnomer.

Faces don't align as such except where waste is

figured in, encouraged in factorials

one had planned so could plot out, and then

so did. I lapse

near niche's absence, yellowing its curl

to fillet age becoming then not young

but tenuous to better straddle value's cusp

and lap at what has come to replicate its place

amongst the system it designed to later make

itself within. The city seeks

its replica be neotenous, its model Swiftian

for fun in how it propagates

or not quite that but, well,

because its lean concept of fun

is pain augmented for the peak

of purpose, levitated high as need

and near as crystalline in reflex I

am tasked to proof it in. Dubai

sent us its yeast

and now alleges something untoward led to that.

It may be true. Florid gestures now abound

where Turing's coins before spelt purity

within the error folded into ethos' now-empty set

where the stock fondant of the ocean rends

the larger will of calculus

milled pure yet from its purer grit

null values marbled all this wasted mire firm.

There are more books than can be read, but not more than can be bought.
Is this the way that capital slays?

No. I think it's words' grand armor.

×

{ }

I was taught to frag then surplus.
I prime some flaw to gain with
It a forge. I huff a tint, then flex
To hustle some hard trusts up.
I have to come with u once more.

A form conjures itself, decides
That it is red. For instance, helots
Are the fleshy part that voids
Count as their fruit. The accident
Of flavor merely proves a serf
Has wished. So wishing isn't cause

I fell unkindly, knowing forts
Hewn from the stooped lean easy.
When delay of cause wins an
End I finish glad. I so rest that way.

House coward.
Prudence tufts.
Use, piled in the far yard, tans

as formlessness descends at it,
a politic. Features began.

Come rub warm your hands in this tint.

To leech from leisure desire just have it.
Leaden as habit, have at it.
Soft becomes dewly lit trials of context.

Though perhaps what has fallen far enough past may bow
into a note, a score totes no sound. Sequence is what gets found.

Counting builds. The numerals that cushion plant flesh climb
the Acropolis. Atop are patient theses.

Figured ache a singeing, the harp contends
each pluck severs credos. It is how lungs lift.

How pliant may a will become and who is it
who slathers grease on wounds who earns this job who stomps

figs soft in that arena dirt who evicts the busts fallow there who
dips his pail in horror's runoff to not slosh the pillage home tell

me who. One who tours
history to sniff out edicts exits trailing scalps glued to his boot.

In frocks and dowdy on couches, repetition paws its snack bowl.
So bronzing melts duration. As digits ticker by on starchy peaks.

I log a curt allowance skimming lean
from later-ons begun
in feal and therein ended.

Coming-to's an end again.
Gives' plum jus belies a loading pond.
Just prove that a man's not.
Just prove that one man's not evil.

We want to go from the evidence back to him.

There were two Tuesdays. George, I know I told
                you, sir, to quit. Quit
                at once. There were in
                the pantry two tin cans
                of pinto beans. There
                were burlap sacks of
                lard to carve. George

      can you dare tell
           me you,
           weak as
           you are,
           wouldn't
           consider
                            gorging yourself
on
      minted leek bisque
      minted quiche
           w/ beaver sausage
      minted *lamb*
      minted butter bibb slaw w/ toasted pistachio
                        pear cider foam?

Who let that boy in
here? Who let that
boy in? I will not
stand for this, this
boy be'ing here. I
will be not, *boy*. An underside of constant flavour is that that

belies reason. See, it decides *for*
the parlor what would rest, wait.
What would sit on an ottoman
stiffly, what would let us say
perch there and absorb some
of Morton Feldman who is in
the room.
George George George, George. Tell us that carpet listens.
We will never believe
it, this is what of it we adore.
Stewing florid poonies, wooding generative plasticity, souring to
many forms of protest among the blanding tidal portents on that
particular brandling Tuesday.
Touring clinic jester-looming
sat us down in mass recliners.
Where were in the room two.

Too in the room were
too boys. Who let too
boys in here, who let
them? George too I'd
bet, I'd bet the weather too

preemptively
understood it
self (that it *is*
pure and mere
condition, that, were one to jolt from fully reclined to scan
the front lawn from the multiple jocular
adjacent angles, the resultant composite
would be no better, *George*, than what
one, reclined fully and peering, craning,
from the supposed comfort of his or her
(or her) seat, could in all probability see,
even considering a gleam
and even accounting for
varied imperfections in the pane (it
*is* a processed home, we know you

know, we've grumbled of little else
while your back was turned, dialing the burner's heat. We do not *want* a stew,

can you understand this please?

Two there. Yes, two. Scurry off and tell
George in a flurry we will haste *away* if
he steers another wooden spoonful near
our mouths. We have our boots arranged
toes *facing* the door beside the doormat, tell him          this.

Accrue use
then hoard
hard labor / In Chanticleer's cellar

I'll fit to pare disgust its nostalgias.
What guff to allow the meager in.
Into *The capitalist's body* we do go,

lavish with our fetishes. A thing so
flush with capital
is endlessly calculable, and as such
knows infinite its unquantifiability,

the sun-weathered Minion balloon
still fat. Foam is purple, need is flat.

When I ask for your hand I really
Mean it.

Waft final, bleak from sculpting a model, I add up all the nuance around me,
in total it so amounts to the winks a flaccid owl doles out. I love it. It is great.

Soon hair let down will feed the certain fire. Boring notes burn all the nicer
the boringer, so he got oily, slathered with lore he'd hewn, for tires love fire

near
completely, inside a left sandwich bag, having smeared goodly my hands to

get rid of it, your answers in sequence await but they're lonely—by burning,
made lonelier. An alley in this city is perpetually aflame. I know it's lame,

saying so. Acceptance can't clip
terror free

from the banality that's binding it. I'm told that is the whole point of terror,
which we want. Now— listen— you can't touch the car door here or here or

there, here's OK, here is better, your experience is pleasure creeping nearer
when your back is turned. I'm only here to help. Flowers gouge out my eyes

because I let them. I can't decide
if I let them

because I want them to or want merely to accept it. If one were to construct
a scale model of scope it would need to be larger for sure. The type of tower

you're into is bleak. You're in it, gazing so, glancing about, regarding, down
like so, I look up there, where you are at, peering up, grinning, up, searching.

So turf is that I
Put beside doing

A mild dream

Farther tours off
Curt a ripe leaf
When simple livid

Beige nouns bruise
Clean but wet
A framer layers it
Power its cant lip

A lake may dispel
Any rim its cutting
Done and a knee

No song it marks

Part of it is here
Part of it is here too

Was it really only the sun

I lost

Menacing semblances

An instance assembles if

Notice is cerulean

Noting takes absence off

Swift rust a sheath draws

Tarred in it all not

Punctured bereft without

Into color

A positive

Sequence ridding favor in

Patterns I left you with

Wishes For

Leave polis lacking

Nonce wild

That what is tidal undoing

Locates a taller object

Upsetting lo

A face coming forward

Leaning atop

Tufts so lithe

Being lit up

Getting til rational means

Plight tones

The treaty before us lies

Begun at tact

Then left to wrinkle

A pink rim and

A hid flank

Low along its cusp

A lot of harm idles

Beside a lofted engine rapt in chrome

To call it gleam

Alone seems novice

But ploy emerges teeming

From where truce encamped

Nearer trickles

Having bled in

Issues a rivulet curates

It takes its places in context

The difference is permission

Trimmed bivouac

Becoming scanter

Among parsimony carved in

Eaves lither overhanging

Dropping stones

Not quite below but

From a flue belief lifts off

An incantation having slid

Upon hovered terrain

Needless at pasturing

Aslump and riper than

Laurel a dunce saturated

Laid out before

Cantor plying egrets from thorny wreaths

Pulses inset with diversion

Lead installed a timbre in it

Brought about where wrought iron

Placates transplants

Though so hollow

As to notice

In pools intent

Tawdry indigo of error

To let down skirts, appeal

To blur daemonwater upon, well, us

Figs drop

Then you trounce on them you don't care

How about a steed or two

Dolor unto tonite's barracks

Suppose twelve squat lines lift

Then hover, rotating, into a shape

What is a shape

Except resistance,

Went ruptures cauls

Accepting cowers

None contains the motion,

Cerulean bother

The cast hasn't mattered

Ungainly thesis of clouds

Flabby ribbons

Angle before us, at a gate, why

Are you here

Teal static

Yes

Certain subtle medium browns,

Similar in bolder blue, then

There's the gray

Given leering balds

Desire

For untoward cant

Is only overripe

In the beforetime

Where

Idle

The humours find it level

It's a want I have about an ease. There is
a simple water I want, I fund want on it, not
touching tho even its wanting, aware of
its yawning presence, the dearth belongs
beneath us, where I keep shoveling lack.
Mist of cool blue coal steaming upwards.
Frack until the berth becomes a bulbous
index. A hand dips into greening waters.

Limit is the essence of a plane. I wish to
lay you down upon the gray fronds of it,
bathic pyres fold heavy wants around it,
trudgeries of a downed drone browning
in red sand. Urgency locates a need that
isles wear upon their seas. Come here, OK.
Limit is where I wish to come upon you.

His nose is wet. The palms collect their
need in pools that stillwater's dowager
becomes. The banks are rifling
thru greasy notes his fur took of for fun.
I have a leaden pellet that bores
thru where it rests. Wetness is
a binary. Yet that green towel is dripping
on the rubber grip of a cartoon
trapdoor poised to pour forever surplus.

×

{ }

I am fine
letting things.

I've made rot.

The terroir, its yesterday's foul. I've eaten the cartoon carcass of a broiled owl,
     and in it confess I
tasted, if not
empire
itself, the fruit one'd think one'd mash into one's turrets. I have come to—if
     not enjoy..., keen
castles' rank flavor, its encoding of pittance, how scented its spackle is,—see,
     it's for sure that
the qua of wealth is the halo
of even the sadder bloods, I
myself have confirmed this, and could relate it to you if you push me on it.
     But rather let us
discuss *feelings*. I have *many*. My microtensions falter before they can
bask in fruition, and unless
ur a *Stupid. Commiedick.* you get that, you intuit a certain purpose within
     anything
repeatable
that bears resemblance to what's most dire among us (we took a poll),
and the general sense is that she acted insensitively to his hostility, which, yes,
     was hostile, but
she acted insensitively. And also in, it can't be avoided saying, a meek way, she
     should have done
*something*, right? The effervescence never
falters right in the earthier temperaments
and I can tell here a certain... toil regards us, from the affrontery, that brass
     goat's
curatory aura,
—you can smell it almost, yes? Yeah, it opened
last week, there was a gala, like, Thursday, but, otherwise, rapt I were,
as if, along the arcade where one feels heat's dank hum almost

fondly, being foretold never I'd falter heavenward, to bask

seemed mild

upon the butcher's gored-up flank.

My name is Chaunticleer,

to-day.

Never am I public, there persists about my placedness a whorl that before, a

    time, two, did swaddle

the barrister's gutwants even, if they nearby passed,

or if, in choosing to pass unlooking, bowed, carp-like, draped as such-so,

a harp within a bespoke jacket

brought to playing by (sigh, they wish)

One's Personal Sensitivity Toward The Poor,

a feel abrading fingerpads which they deem

enough

and good.

But being brought athwart forced, I wonder I ever dulled it, flat as affect

    for inflection. Having

even a need

is of course weak, and coarse. The broad among us wrestle woe, I did mention

I have feelings, this, as such, is one of them, that a count worries internal all

    stout-

hearted persons, it's a ward of encouragement, the route

thin blood tracks abroad the marble that you'd flick it off on.

But yuck to blood.

And bile's passé too.

I

have grown accustomed to releasing—see pigeons hurled off, from a long

    canvas coat—epochs

of self-knowledge, I find it

I guess

tedious, The Baroque gelled right to gutwarmth, a total drag, especially

when conversion's being's meme. The revisionist theme, *It becomes you.* And

    so it does.

One.

I need to rewatch the movie.
People are, like incantations, they move thru
being same as hamburgers, and one can never
have too much *joy* have too *much Of* mild

wishes. The air displaced
by the platter's settingdown went north
and south, less east, none west. West is
where touched first. "I *have, to, tell* you, I
just *have* to" and then the burger's bottom

bun's reflection elastic becomes.
Naturelle is it what's hot, it's new, but not
all's new is hot. Her fingers end in it,
it's hot. But what they won't do it won't
do for her. Around the way, a stench. People
speak. And feet should all be "a pale pink or

beige colour," but they're not, they are busy
with fidgets, ugh, what is use. Going embues.
"That it's a beacon is funny, you know? it's just

that, sometimes—don't fucking laugh. Don't—
it's just that" And off with all's data in pairs.

# POSY CROUCHING AND SMELLING

*Preamble*

Atop the wont's luxury, that man holding his blaspheme.
And under: another who imitates one gathering flowers.

Mild fidgeting whose loaves 'tonation kneads
is salaried tedium.

The duty given is to scrub at philosopher saddles.


*Coda*

He sat at a stoop liquored in mareblood.
He sits still, supposing...

"If a witch
 weren't to melt, she weren't composed of ice-cream."
Before the teasing happily belies want its working

means day eats good
 the artificial covet of besting our heaving salves to.

Figures adore tally. Nevertheless,
I pile approximation near. I cast
allegory as my turf. Then I talk glut rosily.
As I count them one to three
the middle is rude at the extremes who sing.

The please of doing peril is limper
before memory. Two gestures can
loosen empire into dark matter's firmament
of numeral. I peer
toward where fissure's firmness is its will.

Core in value, loud for hire, pouring files
        for likes et al are viable
if the problem is permeability.
The cure is bent by recent fur.
I eat a block of cheese before an algorithm.

Hair glade dewy flume took
me a deficit
pronouncing 'things' wrong not
on purpose but yearling water
trundles over the airy burly tufts

Frowns adorn green things so
what a deed intones
I've earned
such fads as heirs denote
but let cold lofts to dayshift hosts

Cured before, it ate at her no less
for all its dallies,
sore if good a moodlight took on
pewter flakes
upon her tub, the daily facedness of lust

Uncall me then if foils
thrust yet shim a donut, nothing
touched, I've read of halos
that sit on the dead who weren't
if but for the hover but tour alone

The eaten bitemark, those slakes
have rotten life in them
I ate
a half a dome
but I could not find the foam I kneed in

Ideas about the palaces I keep
In tidy files in the back and very
Near a fury I bound to myself
In service of pale want of being. I
Have taken in some wilt and I
Aim still much lamer to become
In precious tones a grayer ease
Befits, like character is destiny. I
Do consider this or that, and I
Think some is good and some is
Bad. I pull rank when possible
To take what is not mine, it feels
Fresh upon the skin to do so. I
Should know. I make complexes
Of the subtle modes I daily feel,
For fun. It means so little to me. A
red bead has now fixed upon me,
Sure to fire. It's hot fun. It means so
Little to me. Force of will impresses
Me.

"Ronald, what is truly unique about
Human culture is. But I disagree. The
Rough draft is that. That's next
Tuesday. Oh. So that's what"

you meant. The desert's lethargy
*urges* the pallor of hostility; there
are specks that, peopled, visit
vice upon senatorial self-image. Tho rare,

toons become damp features the sand
feigns grief for, impounding in dusk
the datum most crisped by then,
a withered gladness over entropy.

Carve downward into the thigh's flab;
flay. Then flay, and enter the banana
by the stem. Fulgent are the
barricade, stresses beading wafts

thinswarm. Ponderosa beguiled him;
my brother'd wanted chicken. How felt
Toledo's coal-orange felt, the blush of
motel-fostered puissance once vacationed.

The suitors align bearing this
fear across their chests painted blue.
The suitors, men or women,
broad in the sad oven of the sun's glee.

In gestalt there's tinder, and to groom is
a plainsong, but effete the jury were, the
dour urges for titling do tend to chafe, it
is no fun
any longer, caring, too demanding of one's vapours which tending must abjure
if to ease, perhaps as bandying a lubed cock warps want sure inward, any want
really, is becoming of juncture, for instance
the camel's hoof upon the sand becomes the sand,
and so here discernment begins. In inns speckling
country foothills painted flatly green feeling happens. And if one ages into want
of excerpted light, it lathed into regular prisms the
floor feels, blindly, and the rug knows
it is August,
so too is the grunt from being fucked hard a minor
acknowledgement of some facet of difference. One,
next. It matters none the color, flame
eats change, makes water of it, this is why a camel can't be torched. Its hair burns,
sure. And, similar, verisimilitude falters at the foot
of the foot of the stairs, maybe a jester
beckons, and suspended in the air's a galleon built of knives,
but who can board it, or would, because who can't? Newton
grew an inch
an hour, it is
how he commanded the physical tones the earth is,
by bending just upon standing and, one, adjusting his pants around flab, jostling
his scrotum and smelling his thumbnail.... There's a
boast about machines, that we should
love them or,
to put it as other, let them
love us, accept unremitting stony adoration and wash oneself

in acquiescence, and it is bold, like licking come from an ass,
and just as gentle, but nothing of the taste of it pertains, how can one remember love if its
lack sells even sand's bounty? Love so wounds the camel. It smiles. It dons a coat of flame,
it smiles.

Air rifles
files, the
tan pond
investing
Huxley's
daily rote
Victorian
empathy.
If he were
to explain
Platonism
gashes us,
becausing
false-item
pathology
of its frail
tenures—
a jazz undo if he lives gamut-furnished and pally in a Soviet rhetoric-bow
&, peeled
against its purchase to expose suet like love is courage's blanching shield,
camphor
arises off
ripe dead.
To inflict sour hearers with whose fur-musket quotes altruism's final tear
is defeatist
& is a bad
goal. But the genuine act ages historicity. So whose girdled, peevish heart
could rival
the mothy
bothering

of papers,
an archive
telling lies
to dull loss of clarity because the beaver pelt feels of it, eachly, per annum.
Being tuff
on futures,
Aldous bet
presciently on synthetics, but his genital census comes in error-bloated—
&, to gnaw
on factual
muscle, if
Thoreau's
pond were nuclear of this feeble being-genre, codices would avail a rabbit
palmed and
jittery because muscle bears yet any year's drone, vatic, furred, in apostasy.

Op. durational becoming, given whatever's pooled, I won't see the cupped
    hands extending toward me. I will
chastise you good I promise. A garment has you, there you go. Sail in jest
    toward Andalusia
you get there soon enough
then palm of many daisies before the yellow peaks, which abound, ahead.
The doctor is fond of you.
Always continues something ahead. I've considered that shame is its own
    distance. Or... duration. I just can't

decide
the two if differ slips of up.
Rifts is all there is, many
so eroded they rise atop
the nearby rifted land. These rifts one must scale
to fumble griefs and also bruisey roses over them.

Fantasia lifts up
them bereft.
Whereas if theater gives you its blessing, leaves for you
baskets of cheddar, shiny lockets, health literature that
means well, lifts you into a saddle and
dandles you an uncle grieves
untold losses and renders lard without even having to ask you
sit up in bed. The geese are at
the park
they do not fly away. Across the smelly pond in crosshairs is a man who's
    rude and gross. He labors to inherit

pain to dole on heirs.
Figurant bugle, delay
the fact within logos,
its bad mystery often
compelling deeds on
the otherwise not so
hurty to do just that.
In hurt's then feel if
their limbs configure
the soul, swollen, sat
upon, and lounges on
to perform its bad doings, being a principal theme.

That the soul is the gout of the self, that is, I think.


Hi debts.
I dial lithe perched on pinked ridges the rain Alain made war from. Need
    bled thru the tourniquets. I let forts
to generals, then let fortune sup its urges from a shallow larder spate of air.
    Oh oh did you ever think of a bad idea? Nearby the bight is sod the tide
retired there, rich in loaves to parcel out

labor where leisure not work eats war.
None manage the rise from puft bread.
But hordes of participants' teeth foam,
Biloxi's unwilling id,
a skin, you can't get off.

I spent
good money on tutorials.

Pertinent cusp,
where limp hastens nearer fitness,
two jousts glisten.
I've sent this... fist thru instance;
so cadence lifts sense

from list to limit's denuded tenses
sifting at cement 'til civic
sand obscures the wars raw imprints.

{ }

×

Then going on,
the lot

Wagner dusted

aloft hung. His

dread
is glib.

His toot burnt said.

{ }

✕

# TO BE VERSUS BEING

*to* C.

A way of costuming myself from doubt

That may be it

It may be that

Away from us the dust in purls lifts up

The white from its flag

This is it if there can be

Any error I might abide

Where gain

Leaves need

I long known toil to cuff my will to win

Enmity I own and so can portion doses

Toxin being a sure balm

To be versus being until

My dar—ling

How

Are you

How

Have you been

Late—ly

I only want for you to bend into my name

Until I can't remember a

Gain

Go past roads dust hung

Up is an act

Going toward care is too

It is in act I

Learned to ease an urge opposes being

So I invite

Urge into

Love's centrifugal curve

Western route that held

Me tighter into us against the outer pull

Of error leaning nearer

To being, to be near act

Bent against the wind's

Arced tug along the curve you cup me in

Gout climes foul hills hung in
jewelly precocious interaction.
Presst, I hand
seams frothed to jocund rage,
blind as water
that voyeurs a promising career.

Then crux's sin is our dominion.
Domination limps on becoming.
As it is, nearby
temperature edicts hills I felled.

You come near my Appalachia.
Thus incurs markings by turns
Illegible and
redacted the cartographic knoll
displays fire's hierarchy, spread
ghastly toward the tune further
on a cliffed populace, portrayed
as opposite the map's rising scenic rifts.

The jewels, I
hand can't inscribe legibly rows
diminutively into my cold horn.

Harpo's latent urge to torch
ignites event, it's heat
that calcified the lung discovered
red in drawer, as if spread defines
every motion. Ceaseless dauphin,

lift gushing its anonymity. Vanity
amasses. To long
for the sea's simmer is weak, I do, I'm weak.

Lather under leaves the fun's tint
a bas contorts allure leaned into
jest, a leavened scent of losses.
I'm who compels the gloss is forgery.

Albeit the foil of tender is bruises.
Currency being choosy but not for who says
dainty jokes that feint at wholeness
having took a run at the spleen's wet marshes.

Use begets forgetting newness.
The noon is low, son, all is while.
A day long past I thought the lawn could solve us.
An atom angles languid while one other's crushed.

Afar, funds impel a bounty

Unwrap your false wrist, reuse

the ace in lamer markets,

There is naught, being Western, useless—

only a matter of repackaging

for store credit (discard the kept receipt)

Unfurling like gay nature's blooms

Credit is the purer simulacrum

Heft denotes… something unpleasant,

the gate's ajar, tufts poke around, and

the asphalt's pores admit only in pools

There's known boon in leveling,

figures to punch in and loud receipts

immediate as tally ascends and so

ascending furls,

The stouter urges even can't too lift,

if viable they gird the roots,

then gild them, and then what?

If gore lifts from its wound,

would it be a healing?

—and hovers there,

would a figure be just a buffer of gore?

—and how to pass an arm thru

to hand over cash

fortify a galleon in doom

let us make the ocean further

I wave a dollar

over bent heads at desks

they look up

for the scent,

—and what now, salable dusk?

Yes. What, and now.

1.

"I think I broke my thumb from hitting you."

"I'm sor—"

"You can't say sorry to that."

2.

This that before us, fulsome, splintered, wandered into,
wanted, O, away a dalliance
'tween resuscitative tut & brow-down kolony trothing,

gas-splet brung out the beaut's gore, two-toned, I wiled,
ungarroted. A sandy therefore-defile.
A never-been Tucson, the warrant's fulgent aerosol

while, finicky, acres burn sorrow whose lake presents the knoll smoke-endured.

3.

Why wouldst one unmurder,

4.

what is done is fun, the past is a jibber that numbs!

5.

Meanwhile, at the dog café,
the phosphorus sausage is sentient: and it wishes

fortune's disease partake of you. That you who sups
could call slimy history none argue.

THE WURST INTERROGATION requires none of you.

Int' weight an arc fainted
Lame graces the face of a
Later knoll to take in too

Tight how in poll my lull
Cleaves issue their rends
Where water pulls gather

Some day will lilt me over
As plan fast ashes nearest
Flame it yes did so etch up

Accede me nohow carries
Droplets up an arc in war
Thru flue I hear the shape—

Air's flute, no, isn't fewer

Through full while lamer reticence
envelops us in patters seeming dutiful
if not morose with residue, like
sulphur's tinge, ajar somewhere further
in still, but brought about as
though a husk enclosed the tender
sense of it, a grant we loosely held
that would allow some being rough with it.
Form honors labor's waste. I left
half an ounce in your attention, surplus
candor catching tone's slow effulgence
as deft; a timbre pleats the thinner air. Up here
I have time. Palmed, stonefruit becomes
estranged from touch as flesh on flesh
wafts up a delicate simpatico wherein
nationstate does not dissolve per se but does
tip inward as the land does slope
approaching valley no water dampens
so does not demark against the ridge
that cuts its shaft then up
through the latency of air's unfeatures
allowing boundary into this inversed
parabola where form can only assert
its formlessness so far. The fruit's cool
flesh feels faintly damp
against the hand's light clamminess
until weighed against the other features,
to offset the body's dark
proprioception involves taring out
the scale for this:

Whatever's further inner
is deeper
not because in possession of more depth
but because the framing of its presence
is so greater
the encumbrance of sensing
is kept truer
because so well impaired.

Gentleness slips over
and over again from
grasp, like fluid cooed
into held form.
It's plastic's long song
that keeps lasting.
Longing comes only later
on. One bruised ledge
to soften under a jumper's
urge to ruins who leak order
I will to steps. I will leverage
process again against
how used this coping is.
A furnace's rank heat
tops out at ten percent
its fuel's core. I fuss its
coals around—a making-sure.

Poor is
mere, I
reason with memory, allow
the fake its plenty. If acre is

still, useful is the measure I
drape to process reason low.

Once a
sum fit
neatly the self's ripe hinge,
a shim of splintered idiom

I'd gathered to be being's
crux, made silly if meant, same as any swear eclipses value

left raw
as oath,
the open vowel of it notes
loss as present, sustained,

that ongoing the that goes
thru if, casting like aslant light's rife by matter it opaques

the then
of doing.
Having done cures wonder,
not what wound it opened,

and so don't propose rift is
culprit. I need. That's cause

enough,
I'm sad
to say. Were my saying a solution I'd have dug clean out
by now, and what to do with
this ill
soil is
all we'd need decide. Is being
poorer cured by love? Can it

be then that one in love can be
merely poor, having so plain a

lack as
cash in
hand yet not in pocket, soft slit a hand slips in and out of,
pragmatic as any definition of

love—
a place
I'd give up glad I found I had it.

The urge to becomes
More than greenery.
I assent to form its curve toward
Naming's shapeliness. Listen to
Before become fungible in prior
A priori as posteriori.
I suppose you're right
There's wastefulness in watering
The ferns at dawn if I don't wake
Naturally then. Late
Night becomes light
Enough. Waste endures us some.

WHITE FLAG

*for* C.

Soft cures

wear dire

handling figures,

turning them over.

Nothing is three dimensional

at once,

to move

is a spectrum of compiling.

Into gain a need leans.

It isn't benevolent how

matter arcs

toward light,

so too

does love

approach calm but only approach.

Less urgent

usually means

nearer crucial,

rich sludge

sags in ripples

away from

though toward me I am

tilting this Nermal mug

concentric alloys of

relent, yes, I

do think

all of being's an error,

I still bend toward

you, this is how

I choose to usurp it.

{ }

×

I forge runes.
I
boast wheat. I dew.

{ }

✗

Inform Kipling anew is the lure
comfort beckons dues with.
Dues build on the prior inroads.
C.f. the war waged on tail-
lights is purer, being eternal for
its form of truth the secure
can love because how sure a lie
cops are. Cops are a white
lie made formal. Being white I
was granted naming rights
to norms. I was gifted a white
sword at birth. The swish
it severs fecund air with I was
told to christen Justice. I
hold the white sword firm up
to my neck. I go about my
days. I hold it taut right up to
my throat as I go about my
business at the bank, beckoned
politely by the teller, or
squeezing produce boldly with
my one free hand, then
putting it back, or gliding past
the traffic stop, solemn,
nodding at a podcast, my long
sword kept poised aloft.
Though my elbow tires I shall
persevere, my hand is
steady, impressing my good luck.

What am I to make of this discomfort, I can't buy it, it just arrives, accumulation
    mounts one of its many thrones
and, what, just... lounges there? I guess. Tidy the bannister, the rage comics drape
    well but please
don't fight me on this, I'm repositioning what's
grotesque for our bettering, to not be better but
to swan meddlingly, the crispness of a subcontract.tiff, one that binds in a
    sprawling manner
that ends in what's by then been beheld awhile.

Decorative feeds press upon wherever we've come to look to, I don't know if
    it's we caused it
so I'll apply withering just in case, it's simple to
undo. A ploughman's platter descends shakily.
OK that's fine by me. Having a flavor is where lots goes wrong, the figures
    my enemies swipe into public
air grieves me
but that's not
all, other things do too, I could list some, make
a list you know, compose some, as on a florid scroll that then would travel
    great distances sheathed some

how, in a, what, vial? No lol it's just held by yarn isn't it, how funny, maybe
    drippy wax presst into a crest's stately
ridges...
but that's all....
Simple. I've felt before a tug I could not locate.
I checked the cabinets, I checked the cupboards, I searched in drawers,
    I checked the pantry,

in short, many places, and yet the tug persisted. Continued on, the tug
    did. It did not weaken
it neither did intensify, but rather steadily it rung. Upon, well, my soul,
    tracing up my leg to the fat bundle

of muscle neath my hocks, settling there, then,
roiling would be a way to put it. The canvas all
at once aflame,
backlit and projecting quite brutal abstractions, this is what I imagine
    for tonite's showcase,

see, when I say abstractions I want to be clear, they are to be only briefly
    abstractions, as all
good arts are,
timely so as a
snipping motion— if not the actual crisp slit in air— imbues with certain
dictates the edgewound that's our form. Swells
the boundary does. Smarts, the skin so feels that was a demo for this
    theory's burnished set.
My feed is there to exemplify this, the images of furry things doing it
    then so. Yes. What else did you think.

It is.
Dictation knows the
Plume adjuncts what
Cannot lesson it that
Blathers. Aluminum.
Bathos means ending
And fortuity embeds such persecution annual,

Pockets enclosing soft uses, that, above,
The bereft lessens. Lust unionized. My
Bent to cleave fortune before obvious
Adults. It will grow
Obvious. It "the"
Has as its dirge it is. What
Turing can accomplish is
Knowing that his sad were
Unimpeachable, and progress be none's cousin.

Yet I am, here, wishing I
Had luck fucked. I
Is plural.
Here clumps
The greens of
Simplegrass, I
That formulae
Better knowing, fully therein,
Lap a wet the leaves get, being,
Bellicose, and, a, as stutterer, a
Figment is both its figure and its issuer.

*Mulholland Drive* posits that Hollywood's the lure of trauma.
You lose the mood sprig flow would gain.
After, we ate calmly noodles. Loot commands a theory of use
flock to it, otherwise, well, worth just sits there, loosely.
Sometimes, an attempt alone's enough to thwart your critics.
Your critics being
inept critics but in other matters, budgeting for instance, not
bad. The crucible torques meat so plump from I guess bones?
Lurid detail casts some important pallor about a comely noon.
Some important pallor conveyed a closed rose to the audition.
A grand thirst not
"for" just cancelled
satiety is merely pure and so the archetype's flexed hand, near,
comes for the thing, imagine its shape, that it has so it has heft,
now isn't that nice?
I'm smiling. Hello. When dual vials pour as one, hi.
Wherever a note ceases fast as if snufft, hello hey u. A real fat
and also cute worm giggles on a hook. What seized it as labor,
this taking-place the cleanly diner serves as a meek, proud act,
a hamlet's treason
accrued relentless fees. I'm told it quaint to pay them. The hurt part
is deep in there under sensing. In there where it really smarts.

Adieu on tour the paler gaffes
have pantone lathed in figure
sifted lest fireplugs spout tone.
Then's rift had sod tossed in it.
Halve as such begun by seeping, so.

    Wafts I file I collate inside I will.

Will u? 'If' uplifts fatal wishes.
I give it 2 months top but lean
with me a moment at the edge,
no figure at end lents the fake limp
if having been named is good. Fine.

    Lakes tint at the pain I've made.
    In this plot leaking faltered loss.

Since error comes tailored lint
is finer easy and then as easy I,
appeased, can make war spout
from any hole a puncture likes.
What spurts a pain knows hurt
is intimate until the hinting's end is.

Immersed in like it really ends mean.

Trust in capital to ungentle any need.
Heaps of Rights invite coring publics.
I welcome in a soft convexity that pools
under sodium lamps sizzling on at dusk.

Infrastructure of distrust, orange dust
singes distance's blurred edges. Time is
too lenient with history. Nonetheless
a given lull may indent a day as gently.

Adjacency labors in green belief;
nearby are bent backs rearing up
then again going low— as pistons do,
—it is thru machinery we collate this,
not via human labor, as though
the meat men wrung sweat from bent
over the machines that built the tools
to make machines were so taken
by the task that none of man remains,
so exhaustive this mimesis, buried in the task.

When a thing is near there is a sense in which
the thing solely can become yet nearer;
sighting is initiative, an ontological arc,
a threshold of what is so just then being
brought irrevocably into being, because
known. Curb labor and then continue
to sweat leisure, let no good lack of work
go undone or, done, go
without laying waste
to lying around in a warm bed.

Time, much like its father, feces,
must go somewhere. It's all about
allocation. I don't know what to do
with it once it
is handed to me. Then it is no longer
near, the touching of the thing
being when belief transfigures into work.
Belief is not what hands do.

Halp abounds. Foul takes continue
taking the water, which is enjoyable,
unto themselves. Profit then results.

Don't let on that
what lives goads
distinct ones into being. There isn't

the time, late the hour grows, as such
it becomes her,

greatness does.

People, you, and
me, in total are a
fireplug of war.
Rainbows bend into our gushes, since
color's spectre's love's the hue of war.

Cameramen are handed flowers just
within the frame.
The lead's blurred face bends toward
and out the lower
edge of frame and
then back in, and if you closely listen
and turn the volume up a bit, you can

hear, faint, his thick inhaling; and one
practically huffs
that daisy in, it's

like, OK, we get
it, you're pleased

and the flower smells nice. It's pleasant.

Enough of this derogation. Clime of unblushing digests,
I ask of you, please remain kind in the way of the hand
That dusts the cherub figurine. The urge to topple
Will cumulus the past. Before I spoke of this,
A jury of your peers and neighbors reached consensus
That your continued restraint had transgressed from *neatly heroic*
To *sinister*, and you hunkered by the fires ceaselessly rotating logs.
Unresponsive migration whispers hewn cubes fractal.
There is not, in this world, so much that resists
If only you adjure your iron gaze, as trained by them
Whom you deride. By old Hollywood. A trope places its cool
Palm on your sandy brow. Consider the grime outlining the bone
Cleaned vacancy, these four reels moved. If I may,
Low on character, admit this foremost issue of resistance:
If put into boxes ever smaller ever smaller, home soon
Is distant as any core from the crust it's known by.

Have I fancied luster's sorrow? Have I been unfair
to you? Have my liens begrudged a funtime? Have I the
rudenesses of dotes?

        I have the receipts, I have toured
inurement, have my teal blazer pressed, I have law's
permeability.
Have I, sullen, leased of ruin? Have I latency to spare? Have I
ardor's crisp investment? Have I invested well?

        I have fees luridly, I have met undoing. My has
contracts. I have encased in toil calming totems of my
abundant gall.

        Aloft even the invect peaks look lifted.

        Has my lasso contingency? Have I streamed the fest
enough? Have I soured blueprint? My has the ring of
jurisprudence to it.

Is the need of words what set the nape-punched joking westerly,
who, having musty texts to import lust with,
who, farther conning, that isthmus labors,
who dressage gets in blunders, trial horse
he abets with, dosing particulate heartward, adoring what's dull
because a question bullies most people, but does he care, he has
answers prepared for such occasion
that what lopes is a wounded character,
and that who rises from the synthetic shrubs, rifle tip ungassing,
and looks pleased must contend with the grasses trounced afoot
and find it good, or find it at least fine,
that to live is just greed,
if greed can ever be just.

Bother lathers a gerrymandered torpor

For georgic pleasantries. Pleasance needs

To bilk fortune of fortune's gilding eaglets;

Who brothers failure surely courts bore.

But same is true success. The baker's foundry

Where what's warm plunks in vats colonels

For fortnights, a battery of alchemical gimps

Emerging volcanic into paper sacks handed sailors.

Simulcast boats toom air's rigorous being-

There, to bother becoming stateside asphodel

In dreary parliamentary evictions of jizz.


One's hands are dyed. If flavor is sourceless

The taster worries and should, the purple

Of lust not being color only, nor operant

Atrophy where drips page roofer garlands,

Thinking glitter absorbs sewage as sawdust

Does vomit. To bother those disconcerted

Bussers whose minds outsourcing even one

Unpurchased image its fragmented sentence,


Even blithe, oblique as loaning a beggar a word,

Requires one to shit clouds that pass as clouds

Just to allow oneself a hope for rain. That it's

Regulation and not pain alludes to separation,

& if eagerness becomes performative, if gagging

Blushes love's final hue, where then does one go?


That bakers knead dawn from just yeast and heat

Is hopeful. The loose flour puffs from cargo holds

Thru zippers, proves that to pat for comfort a shoulder

Does diminish; and the boats alight by confluence,

Hardly courting nearly, coddling its cargo by how

Its keel is, water gaily flayed. The equilibrizing tank

Loves flux. But one wonders does its merry sloshing

Thwart some jagged other's almost-being.... One

Wonders, as if one were water,

Whether one's fear of flux heeds all inertia

But that which loving flux adjusts to love.

# ACKNOWLEDGMENTS

Poems from this book, some in different form or title, have appeared in the following publications: *Bestoned*, *Cloud Rodeo*, *Deluge*, *Dream Pop*, *Fence*, *Mantis*, *New American Writing*, *Prelude*, *smoking glue gun*, *Unearthed*, *Yalobusha Review*, *West Branch*, *Word for/ Word*. My best thanks to the editors.

Credit, for the epigraph's sources, to Giorgio Agamben's *The Coming Community*, Chelsey Minnis' *Poemland*, and Robert Storr's *Philip Guston*; to Carey Mercer ("Claxxon's Lament"), Daniel Lopatin ("Latent with Our Pleasantry"), Drake ("Memory Wound"), James Ferraro ("In Immanence Peak"), Julianna Barwick ("White Flag"), Angel Olsen and Joanna Newsom ("To Be Versus Being"), whose lyrics seeped into lines; to Benjamin Lee Whorf ("Fugitiveness and Proclivity") and Ralph Vaughan Williams ("Dance of Job's Comforters") for the attendant titles.

# THANK YOU

To Srikanth Reddy, for the sight and insight, to Karen and lazenby for the divining, and to Rusty, Ken, Gillian, Trisha, and Omnidawn for the labor to bring it thingness.

To mom, for the unwavering generosity of love. To Corey and Kenzie for all of guidance and growth blood gives. To Cody and Kyle and Bob for the formative. To Justin for the longboys, William for the art unearthing. To Ryan, Anat, Corinne, Meg, Sarah, Iheoma, Claire, Jeff, Carolina for the cohorting. To Matt, to Gaby, to Brigit, to Lisa. To Sue for the kingdom. To Dean for the arena. To GC for the spurring corresponding. To Drs. Fleming, Haven, Lehman, Mackall, Whitbread, Vaughan. To Vikki and Bill. To both Barthelmes, RIP.

To Matt, whose infinite kinship and aesthetic incursion's in every pages' ink. To Caroline, tender usurper, supreme inquisitor, the downest pal, the vital hand in all, none softer than.

Logan Fry lives in Austin, Texas, with his wife, Caroline, where he teaches writing and edits *Flag + Void*.

*Harpo Before the Opus*
Logan Fry


Cover art: Matthew Paladino
"Troys Lament," 40" x 30" x 4"
Acrylic and plaster on panel, 2016
matthewpalladino.com


Cover and interior set in Quicksand and OFL Sorts Mill Goudy

Cover and interior design by Gillian Olivia Blythe Hamel

Printed in the United States
by Books International, Dulles, Virginia
On 55# Glatfelter B19 Antique
Acid Free Archival Quality Recycled Paper


Publication of this book was made possible in part by gifts from
Katherine & John Gravendyk in honor of Hillary Gravendyk,
Francesca Bell, and Mary Mackey,


Omnidawn Publishing
Oakland, California
Staff and Volunteers, Fall 2019

Rusty Morrison & Ken Keegan, senior editors & co-publishers
Kayla Ellenbecker, production editor
Gillian Olivia Blythe Hamel, senior poetry editor & book designer
Trisha Peck, senior poetry editor & book designer
Cassandra Smith, poetry editor & book designer
Sharon Zetter, poetry editor & book designer
Liza Flum, poetry editor
Matthew Bowie, poetry editor
Juliana Paslay, fiction editor
Gail Aronson, fiction editor
Rob Hendricks, *Omniverse* editor & marketing assistant
Clare Sabry, marketing assistant
Lucy Burns, marketing assistant
Hiba Mohammadi, marketing assistant
SD Sumner, copyeditor